Tony HAWK

By Jim Fitzpatrick

The Child's World

www.childsworld.com

Published in the United States of America by The Child's World®
P.O. Box 326 • Chanhassen, MN 55317-0326
800-599-READ • www.childsworld.com

ACKNOWLEDGMENTS

The Child's World®: Mary Berendes, Publishing Director

Special thanks to Tony Hawk and Grant Brittain for their invaluable
assistance in putting this book together!

Produced by Shoreline Publishing Group LLC
President / Editorial Director: James Buckley, Jr.
Designer: Tom Carling, carlingdesign.com
Assistant Editor: Ellen Labrecque

Photo Credits
Cover: Getty Images.
Interior: Courtesy Activision: 24; Grant Brittain: 1, 3, 4, 14, 16, 19, 23;
Getty Images: 9, 27; Courtesy Tony Hawk: 7, 8 (Lenore Dale), 11, 12,
13, 20 (Lhotse Hawk), 26, 28 (Lhotse Hawk).

LIBRARY OF CONGRESS
CATALOGING-IN-PUBLICATION DATA

Fitzpatrick, Jim, 1948–
  Tony Hawk / by Jim Fitzpatrick.
    p. cm. — (The world's greatest athletes)
  Includes bibliographical references and index.
  ISBN 1-59296-760-4 (library bound : alk. paper)
  1. Hawk, Tony—Juvenile literature. 2. Skateboarders—United
States—Biography—Juvenile literature. I. Title. II. Series.
  GV859.813.H39F58 2006
  796.22092—dc22

                                        2006006286

CONTENTS

The World's Greatest Trick

A COOL WIND BLEW ACROSS SAN FRANCISCO'S PIER 30. Tony Hawk, skateboarding's living legend, rolled across the deck of the **vert ramp** during the 1999 X Games Best Trick competition. The crowd of more than 50,000 people was ready. The television camera crews were ready.

Staring from the deck, nearly two stories above

the ground, Hawk eyed the far wall of the ramp as he had so many times before. For more than a decade he had **visualized**, practiced, and attempted what he needed to do to make a "900." That's a seemingly impossible move in which a skateboarder flies off the ramp and spins two and one half times before landing and continuing across the ramp.

Squinting across the ramp Tony faced the

television cameras' bright lights, and dropped in, and a few moments later, landed the 900. Tony Hawk had—again—changed skateboarding forever.

On his twelfth attempt that night, after 13 years of trying again and again, he did it! Tony Hawk added the '900' to his overcrowded bag of accomplishments. Tony shouted, "This is the best day of my life!"

CHAPTER 1

He Just Knew It Was for Him

SOME PEOPLE SEEM TO THINK TONY HAWK MUST have been born with a skateboard attached to his feet, but his mother, Nancy, remembers clearly, "Believe me, there was no skateboard around when he was born." In fact, it wasn't until he was nine years old when Tony's older brother, Steve, let Tony use his old skateboard in the family's driveway.

Tony's childhood wasn't too different from that of the other kids in his neighborhood, although his brother and sisters (Patricia and Lenore) were much older than he was. "We hadn't planned on Tony," explains Nancy. "Frank (Tony's dad) and I were in our 40s, with the two girls off to college and Steve in junior high school and we were going to have a baby! Some might say Tony was a 'mistake' but I

The future "greatest skateboarder in the world" poses at age 10 in a drainpipe near his southern California home.

thought of him more as a 'surprise.'" He certainly did surprise his parents. By his own admission Tony was a difficult child. He describes his younger self as "a hyper, rail-thin geek on a sugar buzz."

As a young boy Tony seemed to be a on a mission to find something or someone that could control his energy. Baseball? Basketball? Traditional sports didn't seem to satisfy him. School was another source of frustration. Even after he was tested and it was discovered he was a 'gifted' student, he couldn't find anything to satisfy his interests nor tire him out. He was baffled until the day Steve returned home from college and dug out his old skateboard. Tony spent the day in the alley learning from his brother how to **carve** and do kickturns.

"It wasn't like some incredible thing, or anything," recalls Tony. "I didn't really care, to me

Who needs ramps? At age eight, Tony gets big air in the alley behind his house.

Sharing Skateboarding with Others

As a teenager Tony Hawk considered the local skatepark his home away from home. Skateboarding became his sport and helped shape his character.

Today, Tony's two greatest passions are children and skateboarding. In recent years skateboarding has grown to include more than 13 million participants, yet there has been a long-standing shortage of public skateparks. In 2002 Tony established the Tony Hawk Foundation (THF). THF is dedicated to developing public skateparks where children can have a safe and legal place to skateboard. Today, through grants and other charitable donations, THF supports programs focused on the creation of public skateboard parks. The foundation favors projects that have strong community involvement, grassroots fundraising, and a base of support from the skaters, parents, law enforcement, and local leaders.

More than 200 skateparks have now been helped by THF. The group's executive director, Miki Vuckovich, explains, "Probably as important as awarding money for skateparks is the technical assistance THF has been able to provide communities around the country. Knowing the foundation is here to help cities has proven to be really valuable to those trying to get a public park built."

the skateboard was just like any other play thing. But then, when I couldn't find anything else to do I started getting out the skateboard and riding around in the driveway for awhile."

CHAPTER 2

Skateboarding Soars Like a Hawk

SKATEBOARDING'S HISTORY TRACES BACK TO the 1920s when metal scooters using metal roller-skate wheels were available in stores. During the 1930s children made their own scooters from wood crates and planks attached to flattened roller skates. In the 1950s metal-wheeled skateboards were available. The sport's popularity really began to surge when clay-wheeled skateboards became available in the early 1960s as the sport of surfing was also becoming popular. The two are similar activities—one on land, one on water. It wasn't too long before 'sidewalk surfing' became a favorite activity, especially alongside beaches in California and Florida.

Skateboarding's next big change came in the

Here's Tony at age 12—already a champion skater—doing a handplant while riding on a homemade wooden ramp.

early 1970's with the invention of wheels made of **polyurethane**, a type of plastic. These new wheels provided a safer ride and a new level of high-performance skateboarding. In fact, skateboarding became so popular during the 1970s that people all around the world began riding. Organized contests and tours of traveling skateboarders sponsored by companies also brought the sport into the spotlight.

This picture of young Tony shows why he was famous for his skinny legs!

Tony got one of those early polyurethane-wheeled skateboards from his brother, and the rest is skateboarding history. As a young skateboarder Tony looked to Dave Andrecht and other local San Diego area skateboarders for inspiration and guidance. His early skatepark experiences were **hampered** by his own body weight. Tony was so skinny that he had to wear elbow pads on his knees and his helmet never fit his head. But the biggest roadblock to his skateboarding was that he didn't weigh enough to generate much momentum—he didn't have enough mass!

Other skateboarders where able to 'get air' and complete other tricks, using the momentum created from their own speed on their skateboard. Tony had to come up with another solution, and he found it in the '**ollie**.' In Florida an earlier skateboarder, Alan Gelfand, had developed a unique trick by stomping on the tail of his skateboard and jumping in the air at the same time. The result of 'Allie's' trick ('allie' eventually became 'ollie') was the skateboard would rise into the air beneath the skateboarder's

Tony's amazing ability to ollie into tricks turned him into an international superstar.

feet, as if it were attached. Tony's ability to 'ollie' into airs at the skatepark lifted Hawk to a new level of skateboarding performance.

Tony's 'ollie' solution wasn't totally accepted by

Here's that kid again—Tony's feet seem glued to the board as he soars above the top of a ramp.

the other skateboarders because his tricks didn't look like everyone else's. Eventually though, Tony's tricks became so impressive, nobody cared that they were different. In 1980, he won the California state amateur championship when he was 12. It would be the first of his many national titles. Everyone began to realize Tony Hawk was a skateboarder like no other.

He turned pro when he was fourteen and by sixteen was considered the best skateboarder in the world.

Over the next dozen years, Tony would enter more than 100 pro events and win about 75 percent of them. It seemed as if he was inventing new tricks every time he rode on the ramp. (A short list of Tony's best tricks is on page 29; for a more complete list, see the Web link on page 31). He combined creativity with incredible athletic ability.

Tony and skateboarding

By the time he was 19, Tony's skateboarding success had helped him buy two houses. At the second, he built a huge skate ramp in the backyard.

suffered through a slow period in the early 1990s. The sport's popularity declined a lot and even the best skateboarder in the world had a hard time making a living doing it. But Tony and other riders stuck with the sport, and the creation of the Extreme Games (later the X Games) in 1995 kept skateboarding afloat. Once again—though he was an "old man" in his 20s—Tony led the way.

When skateboarding roared back in popularity in the late 1990s, huge crowds came to watch Tony's every move.

That Skinny Kid

"I just remember being blown away," recalls Stacy Peralta when talking about the first time he saw Tony Hawk on a skateboard. Peralta, now a movie director and writer, was himself a famous skateboarder in the early 1970s. "Here was this skinny kid," says Peralta, "and I mean really skinny, and he just ripped! He worked so hard at what he was doing, it took him so much effort, that I just thought, 'Oh, we have to get this guy on our team!'"

In the early 1980s Peralta and George Powell created Powell Peralta Skateboards. Their legendary team of pro and amateur skateboarders was called "The Bones Brigade" (Rodney Mullen, Steve Caballero, Mike McGill, Lance Mountain, Tommy Guerrero, and dozens of others were members). At 14, Tony Hawk joined them and turned pro. Before he had his driver's license, he was winning national contests and became recognized as the best skateboarder in the world.

Bryan Ridgeway, Tony's longtime friend and briefly his manager, says, "Tony, from the time he was a little rat, has been the most influential skateboarder in the world. He's not the 'Michael Jordan' of skateboarding, Michael Jordan is the 'Tony Hawk' of basketball!"

CHAPTER 3

A World of Skateboarding

TONY HAWK HAS NEVER SKATEBOARDED IN Antarctica, but he has skateboarded just about everywhere else on earth! The list of places he has visited and skated in goes on and on. He has skated in Europe, Asia, Africa, South America, Central America, and, of course, North America. "It's pretty amazing," realizes Tony, "where my skateboards have taken me. I've been on just about every type of train, bus, shuttle, wagon, car, truck, airplane, or boat that you can imagine. Just to go skateboarding! Skateboarding has just been so important to young people all over the world, and I've been so fortunate to be able to travel and share with them what has been so important to me."

In fact, Tony even almost had the chance to

skateboard in Antarctica when his brother, Steve (yes, the one who gave Tony his first skateboard), visited the cold continent a few years ago. "Maybe I should have taken one of Tony's skateboards on the trip," says Steve. Tony's brother was actually on a surfing expedition at the time. "We ended up in a horrific storm," recalls Steve, "so it was a good thing Tony wasn't there. We couldn't even go ashore for several days and had to remain on our ship for more than a week!"

A few of Tony's most recent skateboarding adventures have taken him to Africa and India

During a 2005 trip to South Africa, Tony showed a group of kids how they could try the "new" sport of skateboarding.

where he has been able to introduce skateboarding to young children who had never seen the sport before. In 2005, in Durban, South Africa, he was able to revisit a skatepark he had helped design years earlier. Tony ventured into the bush to see elephants, zebra, giraffe, and baboons. Afterwards, he and the other professional skateboarders traveling with him, including Andy Macdonald and Jesse Fritsch, performed before huge crowds at the Wavehouse Skatepark.

Most of Tony's travels have been closer to home, however. For instance, he made the X Games his personal playground. This annual summer action sports competition began in 1995. From 1995 to 2005, Tony won 10 gold medals and 18 medals overall. He dominated the vert competition, breaking new ground and showcasing new tricks at almost every event. The X Games helped give Tony national attention beyond the skateboarding world. As he won more and more events, he became recognized by one and all as the world's best skateboarder. Tony was showing that with creativity and hard work, you could go a long way from fooling around in the driveway on your brother's board!

The Summer X Games are held every year at a different location. The Games include events for skateboarders, freestyle BMX riders, inline skaters, and others.

The Numbers Game

Tony's success had a big impact on the business of skateboarding, too. For instance, during the late 1980s and early 1990s, as many as 25,000 Tony Hawk model skateboards were sold around the world each month. Even in today's skateboard market, with so many other models available, Tony's skateboards sell by the thousands. Tony himself has skated on more than 1,000 different boards. He has gone through more than 5,000 skateboard wheels and 3,000 skateboard shoes!

For all of his accomplishments in the 1990s, Tony was named the "Skater of the Decade" by *Thrasher*, a leading skate magazine. "It was the best-selling skateboard magazine, ever," claims *Thrasher*'s publisher, Ed Riggins. "That issue, with Tony on the cover, sold more than 100,000 copies, more than any other skateboard magazine before or since. We couldn't believe it!"

How about the three billion people who watched Tony skate one evening in Atlanta? "There's no doubt it was the biggest audience ever for a skateboarding event," explains Craig Stecyk III, a long-time skateboarder and skateboard writer. The 1996 Olympic Games in Atlanta featured a closing ceremony with an eye toward the future. The organizers asked to

Tony to help them develop a closing ceremony including sports that might someday become part of the Olympics. "Tony designed all the ramps and then performed before the 80,000 in the arena," recalls Stecyk. "NBC estimated their [television] audience to be three billion viewers."

Today, with an estimated 13,000,000 skateboarders around the world, seeing the sport in the Olympic Games may not be impossible. Tony, shown with a 2002 Olympic torch above, says, "USA Skateboarding is working with the Olympics to see if it can happen in the future."

Real Tony . . . digital Tony. Tony Hawk video games (inset) have helped Tony reach a new world of fans away from skateparks.

CHAPTER 4

Video Games and HuckJams

TONY HAWK'S ABILITIES AS A SKATEBOARDER have provided him with the opportunity to share his sport with millions around the globe. There are those who wonder whether skateboarding is really a sport, or not, because it doesn't have rules, there aren't leagues, and there's certainly no umpires. Whether skateboarding is a sport or not, it is fun to do in the video game world. In 1999, Tony worked with Activision to develop Tony Hawk's Pro Skater video game. The result has been millions of video game players, who had never skateboarded, 'skateboarding' on a regular basis.

In 2002, following the development of Tony Hawk's Gigantic Skatepark Tour for ESPN, Tony launched the Boom Boom HuckJam, a 24-city arena

Skateboarding Parent

In addition to everything else they do, Tony's three sons all skateboard, even Keegan (4 years old) the youngest. Riley (13) has competed in a few amateur skateboarding contests, and Spencer (6, with Tony at left) is known for his fearless approach to just about everything. "I'm proud that I can switch from being a skater to a responsible parent," says Tony, "but I don't think I feel as old as other parents."

Actually, Tony's home life is not that different than many other families. With his wife Lhotse, their home has computers, electronic games, musical instruments, and most of the other kid stuff. It's actually Tony's 'office' that's a little different. The home of Tony's company includes its own indoor skatepark. Tony's 'office' is filled with ramps and other elements. The company helps run the Boom Boom HuckJam tours and other Tony Hawk events.

And when you work there, you never get in trouble for playing around on a skateboard at the office!

At this 2004 HuckJam event, Tony soared off this ramp, flying from there to another ramp to do tricks.

tour featuring the best skateboarders, BMX riders, and Motocross athletes performing on a million-dollar ramp system. The wildly successful HuckJam tour has sold out arenas every year as it travels from coast to coast. The 2005 HuckJam featured more shows, more performers, and more non-stop

Though he's an international celebrity, Tony has the most fun just hanging out and skating with his friends and family.

entertainment than ever before.

Despite all travel, tours, contests, and appearances, Tony remains as enthusiastic as ever about skateboarding and his role as unofficial ambassador.

"I never thought that I would make a life-long career out of skateboarding," says Tony, "I'm pretty happy with the way things turned out!"

Tony Hawk's Skateboarding "Firsts"

In his amazing career, Tony Hawk was the first to perform dozens and dozens of tricks. Here are some of the most famous:

1980 backside varial
1983 frontside 540 – rodeo flip
1984 airwalk-to-fakie
1985 720
1986 indy 540
1988 stalefish 540
1989 ollie 540
1990 frontside body varial revert
1992 360 flip mute-to-fakie
1993 cab frontside blunt revert
1994 540 board varial; kickflip mctwist; switch nolly heelflip indy
1995 cab body varial heelflip
1998 varial 720
1999 900
2000 frontside stalefish 540
2002 360 varial mctwist
2003 cab frontside hurricane-to-fakie
2004 shove-it fakie feeble grind

GLOSSARY

carve make the skateboard turn left or right by leaning your body to one side or the other

hampered held back, prevented.

ollie a skateboard jump accomplished by stomping on the tail with the back foot while lifting the front foot from the nose

polyurethane a type of durable plastic that is used to make skateboard wheels

vert ramp a U-shaped structure on which skaters ride back and forth, often flying above the vertical ("vert") sides of the U

visualized pictured in the mind

BOOKS

On the Halfpipe with Tony Hawk
By Matt Christopher
(Little, Brown, New York) 2001
This book describes Hawk's climb from scrawny kid to skateboarding champ, with emphasis on his family and friends.

Tony Hawk
By Raymond H. Miller
(KidHaven Press, San Diego) 2004
This book focuses on how Hawk's creative and dangerous moves have changed the sport and inspired a new generation of skateboarders.

Tony Hawk: Chairman of the Board
By Steve Pittman
(Scholastic, New York) 2001
This book follows Hawk's great career since he turned pro at 14, became world champ at 15, and through his revolutionary 900 at the X Games.

Tony Hawk and His Team: Skateboarding Superstars
By Lita Sorensen
(Rosen Publishing Group, New York) 2004
Hawk's astonishing career in skateboarding is covered in words and pictures. This book also includes a brief history of the sport and features on female skateboarders and basic skateboard moves.

WEB SITES

Visit our home page for lots of links about Tony Hawk:
www.childsworld.com/links

Note to Parents, Teachers, and Librarians: We routinely check our Web links to make sure they're safe, active sites—so encourage your readers to check them out!

INDEX

ABOUT THE AUTHOR

Jim Fitzpatrick has been an active skateboarder since 1957 when he first nailed his sister's roller skate to a board. He was the editor of Transworld's Skateboarding Business magazine and he founded the International Association of Skateboard Companies in 1994. 'Fitz' is currently vice-president of USA Skateboarding. He still skateboards every day, and lives in Santa Barbara, California, where he goes to Santa Barbara Montessori School (he's the principal!) with his three grandsons.